dark alphabet

CRAB ORCHARD SERIES IN POETRY

First Book Award

dark alphabet

JENNIFER MAIER

Crab Orchard Review

&

Southern Illinois University Press

CARBONDALE

09   08   07   06   4   3   2   1

The Crab Orchard Series in Poetry is a joint publishing venture of Southern
Illinois University Press and *Crab Orchard Review.* This series has been made
possible by the generous support of the Office of the President of Southern
Illinois University and the Office of the Vice Chancellor for Academic Affairs
and Provost at Southern Illinois University Carbondale.

Crab Orchard Series in Poetry Editor: Jon Tribble
First Book Award Judge for 2005: Jason Sommer

Library of Congress Cataloging-in-Publication Data

Maier, Jennifer, date.
Dark alphabet / Jennifer Maier.
    p. cm. — (Crab Orchard series in poetry)
    I. Title. II. Series: Crab Orchard award series in poetry.
PS3613.A34934D37   2006
813'.6—dc22
ISBN-13: 978-0-8093-2726-3 (pbk. : alk. paper)
ISBN-10: 0-8093-2726-0 (pbk. : alk. paper)   2006004979

Printed on recycled paper. ♻

The paper used in this publication meets the minimum requirements of
American National Standard for Information Sciences—Permanence of Paper
for Printed Library Materials, ANSI z39.48-1992. ∞

For Frederick J. Maier, 1940–2003

and Marjorie Wilson, 1902–2002

Who, in spring, can bear to grieve alone?
Who, sober, look on sights like these?
—LI PO

We are always entering Paradise, but only for a moment.
—W. H. AUDEN

Contents

Acknowledgments

The author wishes to thank the following publications, in which poems in this collection were previously published, sometimes in slightly different form:

Mississippi Review—"The School of Weeping," "How Love Forgets"
Poetry—"33"
Midwest Quarterly—"Hymn to St. Agnes"
Pearl—"Love at First Sight"
Dream International Quarterly—"I'll Be Seeing You," "Girlie Show"
IMAGE—"Stone Tool," "Eve's Menstruation"
Negative Capability—"Vegetable Man"
Grasslimb—"The Suicides"
The Comstock Review—"The Mergansers"
SWINK—"Happiness Is Being Danish"
Kalliope—"Live Oaks, New Orleans"
Poetry Daily—"Happiness Is Being Danish"
Taproot Literary Review—"Waiting at the Neptune"
theotherjournal.org—"Lot's Wife"

The author is also grateful for grants and awards from the Seattle Artists' Trust, the Academy of American Poets, and Seattle Pacific University. This support has helped greatly in the completion of this book. Thanks finally to many friends who have offered advice and encouragement along the way, among them, Madeline DeFrees, Mary Jo Salter, John Hollander, Donald Hall, Lynn Emmanuel, Gary Gildner, Fred Chappell, Jefferson Rice, and James Fritz.

one

Happiness Is Being Danish

says the license plate frame
of the sky blue compact
in front of me at the stop light,
and I think, well, what chance
did I have, with parents like mine—
French, and Irish, and German—
and under the harangue
of the windshield wipers,
I can just make out the sighs
of my unhappy chromosomes,
forced to perform their slow minuet
in green tights, to the strains
of martial music.

And these others,
waiting at the intersection,
I'll bet they're not Danish either
and never will be—exiles, all of us,
behind the razor wire of "Being,"
a state that precludes *becoming*,
by act of will, or the usual consular
channels; required to declare
Either/Or when we yearn to settle
freely in Both/And; a dilemma
understood by no one

better than Kierkegaard,
saddest of Danes. See how he labors
in line behind us, alone
with the problem of Being,
weighing it over and over

in the long, red light of sacrifice,
looking up, now and then,
from his notebook
to remember Regine—

how they'd once danced the Hopsa
in the Town Hall Square
then stood, hand in hand,
in the unequivocal light
of the Copenhagen winter, happy
to be Danish and in love,
with blue sky ahead of them,
waiting for green.

Love at First Sight

You always hear about it—
a waitress serves a man two eggs
over easy and she says to the cashier,
That is the man I'm going to marry,
and she does. Or a man spies a woman
at a baseball game; she is blond
and wearing a blue headband,
and, being a man, he doesn't say this
or even think it, but his heart is a homing bird
winging to her perch, and next thing you know
they're building birdhouses in the garage.
How do they know, these auspicious lovers?
They are like passengers on a yellow
bus painted with the dreams
of innumerable lifetimes, a packet
of sepia postcards in their pocket.
And who's to say they haven't traveled
backward for centuries through borderless
lands, only to arrive at this roadside attraction
where Chance meets Necessity and says,
What time do you get off?

What It's Like

Not like a brocade studio
where you sit with Brahms
and a picturesque, complacent cat
to wait for plums,
ashen with ripeness and already cold,
to roll into your apron;
more like a journey across landscapes
neither hostile nor welcoming,
with one horse lame
and the wagon listing on a mended axle;
lost, and wondering why you've come,
poorly equipped,
with the flour gone to maggots,
and no promise of arrival—
stopping now and then to heave
some dear cargo—a harpsichord?
What were you thinking?—
off onto the wheel ruts that disappear
behind you. You promise
to come back for it but know
a word outlives its usefulness,
and metaphors are last year's
patent medicines;
so you roll on and dream
of the reaching sea, of the bright dust
waiting in rivers, the first quench
of oranges on your tongue.

Pearls

for James and Jean

When you were three, and I was still a long way out—
miles, yet, from the dry shore of this world,
your mother knelt in the scorched grass
of the front yard and told you how the oysters
toiled for years and in secret to smooth each grain
      that breached the fortress shell
          and hurt the soft inside.

    This I remember clearly,
though you will say only how the scent of lemons
and wild thyme rose from the San Gabriels
behind the house, and how, when you were seven,
nine, thirteen, and I was coming in fast—
    a burning message in a bottle—
        the pearls slept

    in their hinged box
beside the bed, where through long, bad
afternoons, death sang to her in a foreign tongue,
and the part of you no one could touch grew nacreous
and rare, sealed against the red tide rising
    around you, like the tide
        that saw me in and marked

    my Western course. Then,
as the fledgling swift remembers Argentina
from the nest in our back yard, so I remembered
my way forward to you, and you to me; so that night
when they called to tell you it was their sad duty,
    somehow, between the bloodstained
        mattress

and our green season,
you remembered the pearls and dropped them
in your pocket, as if you could harbor beauty
against some day you could not imagine,
except that you felt it coming, round
    and heavy in your hand.

Live Oaks, New Orleans

They square off along Napoleon avenue,
opposing armies of dark women, leaning out
so far their branches meet at the top, like hands
grabbing fistfuls of tangled hair;
and some of them are old, with the thick,
scarred trunks of Storyville madams, and
roots so strong their suck heaves
up the sidewalk like so many broken
saltines. And some are young, with the
straightbacked bodies of girls who dream
of horses and the brown arms of neighbor boys,
but underground the red roots grow together,
fuse in a living circuitry spun deep and
stronger than the whims of emperors, as if
they've known all along that earth's the right
place for love, as though, planted in battle lines,
they incline toward the circle, and hold it open,
vaulted and welcoming.

Fortune Cookie Triptych

1. Answer just what your heart prompts you

And shut up about the rest. Remember,
here you are both the star witness
for the Prosecution, and the grave Defendant;
the federal agent in the blue serge suit,
and the tiny housewife with the bloody scissors
in her handbag. Best to stick to the facts—
Where were you on the life in question
and can you account for your movements since?
Don't worry; the heart is a deft inquisitor,
and you have only to answer truthfully:
How well did you know the Deceased,
and were there any enemies?
Who but you had motive and opportunity?
You may wish to explain that you have been framed
in a plot so convoluted that even you
gave up following, or to plead not guilty
by reason of amnesia, self-defense,
chronic sanity. Perhaps you had only meant
to frighten yourself, and certainly
you were desperate, having squandered
your fortune on pinochle and cheap dinners out.
Be silent. Turn, face your accuser,
and though everything you say
may be held against you, answer now,
just what your heart prompts you:
the truth, small or large, that's yours alone—
that crisp, sweet utterance,
your pardon.

2. The World waits for Talent with open arms

(after the ample nudes of Fernando Botero)

in her suite at the Metropole, where,
at twenty past seven, he is five minutes late.
How lovely she looks watching at the window,
with her peignoir the sheerest of cloud cover,
the balms of the Orient scenting her highest peaks.
She tries not to think about the others—
that upstart who scribbled, near the end,
"The world is too much with us late
and soon"; those cracks about her "broad,
ungirlish waist," her diamond girdle.
And Talent? Thin with desire he paces
in his garret. He has waited forever,
and now his moment is at hand—
for had they not agreed to meet
at half past nine under the big clock
at the Gare de Lyon? He knows
he is not the first to laud her porcine beauty,
but he shall enthrall her with the taste
of his round vowels, his mandolin's
dark honey. She will lick it from his fingers,
rocking and squealing beneath the prurient moon.
Prudent, he'll tarry awhile in her embrace,
knowing that others have too often
been ahead of their time. He cannot see
that the World has already turned away
from him, toward the shy Colombian
who has brought her supper on a tray.
She knows he paints a little in his off hours;
tonight she will take him in her ample arms
and make him immortal, and he will paint
no one else forever: the World *en deshabille,*

turning around in her darkened chamber,
to fix him, the love-struck Botero, in her hungry
and sensuous eye.

3. Don't be hasty; Prosperity will knock on your door soon

You've been waiting a long time, I can tell.
Now, your carnation is limp and brown
about the edges. All day there have been false alarms—
this morning, the tall man with the black valise
who delivered your education, from Aardvark
to Zydeco in 12 slim volumes; and later,
the harried blonde who rang the bell
and took off, leaving your happy children
on the doorstep in a willow basket.
Just moments ago you wept with joy
to hear Prosperity fumbling at the back door,
but it was only your lost dog scratching
to come in. Now, who can console you?
Not even the postman with his fat yellow
envelope, and certainly not I, rattling on like this
when you would rather watch out the window.
Relax. We are all hungry. Pick up the phone
and soon, a young girl in a baseball cap
and red satin slippers will appear
at the door, her cheeks round as moon cakes,
and in her hands a strange and luminous bounty:

golden egg roll,
delightful chicken,
lucky noodle #4.

Thank her, and though you may be famished
in an hour, feast now, without haste,
upon the dim sum of sufficiency,
the sweet and sour banquet
of Enough.

Lot's Wife

It didn't take a white-hot whirlwind
to set me down for good
on this smoking plain;
I was turning hard already—
tired of the edicts and injunctions,
of following my husband's
righteous backside.
I wanted to stay put.
I had friends here, raw
as unbeaten linen, but kind
in their way. I stand facing the village.
It is raining ashes. The groans
of our dying neighbors fall
softly, like the rain.
A few stumble from caves,
alive, seeking water.
Wait till they find me!
It will be awkward at first—
they'll marvel, then keep away.
I won't mind; I am at home
in my mineral skin
and not alone.
Mornings they seek me
in the sulfurous pasture,
the ones who never ask why.
I know them by their sweet breath,
their questing tongues.
I grow thin in the middle.
They have consumed my heart,
but I will become part of their flesh
and part of my people forever.

Very soon I will break in two,
my feet dissolving into this cursed
ground along with my name,
my dry eyes staring straight up
into the dry eye of God
without blinking.

Some Consolation

Travelers heading east along I-90 near Yakima have reported seeing the face of the Virgin Mary on highway road markers.

    Remember angelic visitations?
In the old days you could just about count on them
when, forlorn or wrongly accused,
or when your heart had been callously broken,
you'd look up and there,
grave and courteous in the foyer,
a man with gilded, improbable wings
would hand you a golden scroll,
and you'd feel better for a while.

    Gone too are the days when the Sprites
still made house calls, when, toiling for weeks
on a fisherman's sweater for your college boyfriend,
you'd wake from a fevered sleep to find
it finished in golden thread, with a note
in tiny handwriting saying, *Have a Nice Day!*
tee hee tee hee tee hee.

    Of course, Fairy Godmothers don't
come around much anymore;
while you sort lentils in your burlap housecoat,
they're carousing in the Florida bingo parlors.
And to whom can you complain? These days,
you can't even reach the Muses
on their cell phones.

Now, it is dawn
in a fretful millennium, and we are ready
for sleep. No wonder we watch the skies
for celestial taxis and have whistled in the night.
No wonder we've seen the face
of the Madonna

　　　in the rusting frescoes
of freeway overpasses, to her left,
a field of dolorous sunflowers, to her right,
the beckoning off ramp, to which she gestures
tenderly with a promise for you alone:
Food/Fuel/Shelter : 300 yards.

Vegetable Man

New Orleans

At the corner of Desire and Piety
I see a sign, crowning a rusted pickup,
GARDEN VEGITABLES
the "N" three painted string beans
and a scallion "I."
Below, bright arrows spark
a stenciled proclamation:
Wundrous Carrots, Bogalusa Peach
My Wife's Okra, but it's the
Creole Toms that catch my eye.

He sees and calls *Hey Baby where ya been?*
and I smile into a face like furrowed peat,
lit by a yellow burning
underneath the dark.

I pick a Creole from the banked display.
Last of the season, he says
and I feel it
massive,
ponderous,
filling my palm like something's heart.

He hoists another with his knife point,
splays it on his knee.
The flesh is sweet, he says laughing
as the juice
like tinctured sun
drips from our chins.

For three crisp bills
he swaps a sack
as heavy as an infant
and waves me down S. Piety,

laughing and hungry for tomatoes,
as cicadas whisper charms
against October and six o'clock drops
softly into night's black loam.

For Gravity and Against

The lake is a murmuring woman,
pacing, wringing her hands.
It's the moon's doing.
What does she know
of trouble and consequence,
fat meddler, about to calve?

2.

A heron stands on a piling,
gaunt, morose as Lincoln
in photographs. His eyes
have evolved to see under
the surface, even as he keeps
a level head. He stares into the water
until he has become stillness itself,
then rockets downward, ignited
by a silver flash.

3.

The fish do not think about the moon
or its light, curving through dimpled space.
For them the truth is weightless,
and death only a slow rising—
sun in the open eye,
black hole of the heron's belly.

4.

A woman stands with a hose,
watering the lawn in her slippers.
Gravity presses down on her head,
pinning her to the map of the world.
Last year her son drowned at a picnic,
yet she does not fall through
the crust of the earth.
Under her feet the atoms push back,
bound in their electric need.
Spray from the hose falls to earth,
and a vaporous spectrum floats above
like the small soul of water.
The heron rises in his ponderous
flight, laboring heavenward,
and the blades of grass grow up
through all that has fallen down,
reliably as soldiers.

How Love Forgets

It happens inevitably, invariably, in spite of you.
How could it be otherwise, when nothing will cooperate?
Will the world stop practicing her slow pirouette, unfix
her green eye from that of her fiery love
and weep with you?
Will April lay down her xylophone
and pick up the cello?
Or December go gravely in his mourning coat
without his white gloves, his diamond tiara?

Who will share your hamper
at the Picnic of Sorrows, savor your store
of preserved sweetgriefs and piquant joys?
Not Nature,
She is engaged elsewhere
coaxing a bean sprout from the ground
or a python from its glistening egg;
not your friends, who dine wholesomely
on bread and apples, or your dog,
who can digest only the Now.

Perhaps tomorrow,
affronted by the impertinence
of a summer morning, you'll carry
your broken heart to the shore and heave it in—

On the sand, women raise and lower
flowered umbrellas, and in the water,
old men in voluminous bathing trunks bloom
on slender stalks.

It makes a small splash, like Icarus
drowning,

a splash no one notices,
distracted in unison by something each
is starting to recall—
the scent of *White Shoulders* on a cocktail dress,
the taste of salt on young skin—
something ground smooth and harmless as beach glass
on the sea bed of forgotten things,
in its crenelated caves,
its dark fronds waving.

two

Waiting at the Neptune

H. K. H.

I see you in the lighted ticket window
like you'd been assembled in there,
a Spanish galleon in a bottle,
the eight months of me carved out
in front, like a wanton figurehead.
And I see the college kids
lining up

    down 45th, blue
under the neon trident. They
are about to graduate,
about to marry each other
and stop going to movies, but first
each boy must slip this dollar
through the glass, and you,
spit out the tickets
like a purple tongue.

    Only then will they begin
moving like unwary swimmers
out of the blue April night into
the seascape lobby,
making their way blind
down sloping aisles
to velvet-covered springs,
and waiting,
while I bob inside you,
for the parting curtain,
waiting, each of us,
for our sad or happy story.

Cherries

When I think of my mother's bad brother Jack,
who got thrown out of San Francisco in 1956,
and later, drove a yellow cab with a .38
and a fifth under the seat, I don't think
of the day they found him, crumpled and
bleeding, a bruised fruit on the back porch,
the dark stone still lodged
in his heart.

I think of the day he took my squealing,
three-year-old body in his manicured hands
and raised it—past the twin sequoias
of his planted legs, past the blue dagger
tattoo and the diamond stud—into the cherry
tree, then stood there, holding it over
his head like a loving cup, saying,
SHUT UP AND LOOK.

I'd studied Abraham's face in my
picture bible, the same black beard, and Isaac,
his sacrifice, the dagger plunging down
before the angel grabbed it just in time.
It was July 4, 1964, in Yakima,
Washington. The parade was off; women
were still wearing black for the President,
like he was their own boy.

So it wasn't for the view he raised me
flailing and shrieking, to the sun and the
blue sky crazed with branches, then stood there,
frozen, until my mother came and lowered

his arms. He wanted to show me something
good and growing, consign me to
the paradise at hand, the only one he
thought worth reaching for.

And later, when he placed the chocolate cordial
on my palm, and my shocked tongue found
the cherry, cauled in its murky liquor,
like Isaac, I forgave him, knowing, then,
that love was my thrilling and hazardous object,
something to take warily in my small hand
against the day it would come back to me,
too sweet and oozing red.

Hymn to St. Agnes

She was thirteen when the offer came;
he'd watched her with her mother at the Tiber
beating linen on smooth stones,
charted the progress of her swelling breasts
and marked the cresting of her hips.
Who could believe her luck?
A Roman and wealthy, besides—
the neighbors made blood offerings to Vesta
but I hid in the cellar, praying for miracles
You see, there was a complication:
I'd pledged my virginity to Christ
she was already married, as it were.
Besides he was ugly, and older than my father—
Her parents were reasonable people;
they promised anything, and only starved her
as a last resort. *Each day I begged a sign*
or an explaining angel—
But the suitor demanded due process.
It was a bad time for recalcitrant virgins;
Diocletian had ordained himself a god,
and the magistrate was weary of the provinces.
Some said she got off lightly, just a small
execution, with family and a few close friends.
So when the day came, she was only
the least bit terrified. *I knew the Lord*
would change me to a dove. (That being vain,
a wren, a finch perhaps—)
The soldier pried her small mouth open
to accept the blade. *I waited to climb the wind—*
joking her jaws were tighter than her thighs.
to soar on crystal filaments, as sure as grace

and higher than the flames of martyrs—
Then, cradling his sword on her incisors,
sighed (with an admiring glance at her bodice)
that the young ones were the hardest,
whereupon, he thrust with all his might
I felt a transformation—
while she flopped, drowning,
a scalding lightness—not of air—
and the furious rush of waters—and
dropped, like a piece of linen
among the river grasses,
surprised by gravity
and the weight of wings.

Sliver

The moment I open the car door
and the jar of raspberry jam tumbles
out of the grocery bag and shatters
on the pavement, and I yell *No!*
then kneel down to gather it up,

I know, even as the shaft
of glass enters my thumb
and the red blossom forms in its wake—
I know I'm getting off too easily,
that everywhere, people are broken
for less.

I think of the lost prospect
of joy on the tongue,
of the sun and rain,
so much rising and falling down,
of the deft, inscrutable labor
of bees—

sweet irretrievables,
humped now like some vital organ
on the sidewalk, each tiny seed
a root, a harvest,
innocent as the daughters
I never had,
who come quietly,

cradling small bowls,
until they are standing
on tiptoes before me, leaning
deep into thorny stalks, reaching
with red-stained fingers,
each for her ripe desire,
and I, no profligate, am calling
from a window,
Don't fall, don't fall.

Blue Willow

"The design, first produced by Josiah Spode in the 1770s, depicts a charming Chinese legend.
A disapproving mandarin pursues his eloping daughter, only to see the maiden and her lover transformed
into birds."

I used to think if I stared long enough
I'd find my way in—
awake in that round world of bone-bleached
seas and indigo geographies, far
from the chronic malice of the supper table.
Breathed in by the four winds,
whose names I'd learned at school,
and whispered out,
I would drift down
more quietly than consolation
and lighter than the bones of birds.

The willow would receive me,
her roots, like my grandmother's hands
her fronds, like the exquisite,
backward-arching fingers
of Siamese dancers, inclining
toward the Imperial Palace,
in which the stricken mandarin,
having dispatched his boatman
and dismissed his counselors,
paces in his chamber,
stopping now and then
to swear a monarch's oath:

Yea, sharper than a serpent's tooth
a thankless daughter

Outside
the princess and her secret lover
still quiver from the transformation—
was it terror or desire that in an instant
fashioned flesh to wings,
filling the bones with wind
and throats with the laughter of trees?

And now,
what art, what accident
detains them, fixed
between desire
and flight, between the willow

and the border's
wild blue maze?

In a Power Outage

To the woman—a woman, certainly—
who, shivering sinew-trussed in her bearskin
apron, first looked at the mountain sheep
and said, *Her fur grows like mine,*
but warmer; I'll snip some off but let her
keep her skin and so preserve two lives
in one, I lift my glass.

　　　And to her sisters, who puzzled centuries
by the still-green fire, twisting and pulling
and knotting and singing a new grammar
and syntax of hair, and to her, who
fashioned two arms and a hole at the top,
then gave it—why?—to the one who warmed
her stony bed,

　　　I am your grateful daughter. Tonight,
snug in my mail-order cashmere—*"two-ply*
and soft as love"—I know there is one thread
between us. I feel its tug, raveling these lines
by dying flashlight, a steady heartbeat quickened,
like my own, in the pardonable theft
for snow at the bone.

Eve's Menstruation

It started four weeks after the Edict:
a gripping in her belly like the cinching
of rushes; then a churning weight, as on the third day
when they ate stones from hunger, and later,
    when they shared the first green fruits of exile.

    And when the blood came, dark
like damp earth, then bright as the juice
of pomegranates, it came to her alone, the mark
and injury of separation, and she thought,
    How can Death be far behind?

    She had seen death, and blood, when starved
past reason on the fourteenth day, they snared
the leopard who'd bathed with them in the lagoons
of Eden and marveled when remembering
    brought water to their eyes.

    The blood returns with each ripe moon,
five times now. They no longer stroke the animals
as they die, asking forgiveness. Each day
she sets out early with her basket; each day
he returns late with his bow, the sun red, sinking
like a wounded deer; the moon rising,
    sharp as bone.

33

The astrologer says that this
is the age of portents—
repeating digits, product of primes,
the round fulcrum from which
one surveys the twin planes
of fortune and adversity,
and as she speaks I see myself
standing, one foot planted squarely
on each three's arching summit,
looking East for my joy
and West for my sorrow,
craning forward and backward
along this meridian, as if I could
map the granite face of 44
or ride the treacherous
currents of 22, back
to the land of single digits,
where I learned that Christ
was crucified at 33,
the right age to die I thought then,
a number distant as
the seventh continent, where,
like Commander Peary, I would
leave my mark, raise
the flag of my small nation;
but first I would find shelter—
the way, even now, I'm
gathering stores for the day
I may un-hitch and topple
one of those threes,

then climb into its scooped chamber,
where for one, repeating moment
I'll rock and rock

Chaise

When the man called this morning to tell me
the store had sold the impossibly beautiful art deco
camel-hair *chaise*, the one on which the Siamese
called Simone—a name I have always coveted for myself—
lay curled like a perfect smoke ring rising
from two painted lips at the *Deux Magots*
one day in 1928;

the chaise I had foolishly placed on hold,
knowing that even at 60 percent off, I might, for the same price,
simply start my life over in Prague;

the chaise I knew would never fit
through the door of my tiny apartment, and if by some miracle
it did, would stand there regal and perplexed
as Grace Kelly at the *Rock N' Bowl*—

how could he know that with it he'd sold my Past?
the couch where, as Colette, I'd stared down desire
with my amused and pitiless eye;
where, as Jean Rhys, I'd hid hung over
in its circling arms, a packet of *Gauloises,* a pen,
and a razor beside me.

And how could he know he was selling my Present,
too, the warm, desert mount waiting at the corner
of 9th and Pine to carry me over the border
of this harried afternoon, into the Bedouin night,
far from these clambering tribes whose ways
are not my ways?

And did he stop to think for one minute that,
worst of all, he'd be selling my Future? The one
with the small Greek Revival house in which
the chaise would look *perfectly lovely!*
where I would recline, safe

from the wolf that stalks at my side, happy
that I regretted nothing, least of all buying the chaise—
a sacrifice, to be sure—but which, looking back,
had proved the wisest of investments,
a bargain, certainly, at twice the price.

Paris, 1936

After a photo by Brassaï

The couple in the carnival swan boat doesn't see
the camera, which has captured them, mid-kiss,
at the height of their aerial arc.
They are young, at home in this fragile gondola,
with its hull thin as a Sèvres finger bowl and dented
at the prow, with its looping neck and staring,
painted eyes. She leans back in the stern,
smiling, her own eyes closed, her lips open
to his like the borders of a friendly nation.
Standing, he bends down to her, easy as Charon
in his tight shirt and natty trousers, his hand
resting lightly on the carriage pole.
Behind them, the sky is clear and the sun
stains the ground with spreading shadows,
and somewhere, you can be sure,
an old man is calling, *Look out!*—*it's reckless to fly,*
backward and standing, in a gilded teacup!
but they are deaf to warnings, fixed,
in the high, interminable instant of the kiss,
weightless, before the blind rush to earth.

Girlie Show

Last night she came strutting
across my quiet stage of sleep like
the stripper in that Edward Hopper
  painting,

  dipping and grinding
on gams that mean business, trailing
that long scarf behind her
  like a gill net.

  I am the girl reporter in the third row,
making notes with a giant pencil, while the saxophone
yowls from the pit, and slowly, slowly, she skins
  off a glove, tossing it

  like chum to a man with your own feral
mouth, the same mouth that now, asleep beside
me, puffs out small breaths, smoke from the engine
  that has long since

  carried you out of town,
into this dim theater, here, to the place
next to mine. The cat stirs in the hollow
  between

  us as the glove finds your hand.
In a moment, you'll make toward the stage door.
In a moment, I'll rise and put the coffee on,
  but by noon

I'll be awake and dreaming,
my arms straight as compass needles
trained on the Western sea, my feet dancing
    through Milwaukee,

    through Fargo and Cheyenne,
each town an exclusive; each night an ocean
with its own band of oysters, its chorus of high
    kicking stars.

Vintage Nudes

Hard to imagine them now as someone's
guilty pleasure—
these corn fed pixies and teasing vamps
cavorting in jazz age boudoirs.
We want to avert our eyes,
slip quietly out Desire's half-open
door, abashed to have glimpsed
Grandma, young and half-naked
in there.

Here one sits in baggy satin drawers
at the edge of the bed, cradling
her kitten, waving its paw
for the camera. And here,
a "Parisian Beauty" demurs on a couch
behind a fan of peacock feathers,
its hundred eyes blue
as the Georgia dusk.

Even the Egyptian slave girl
with the serpent arm bands, hands
raised, fingers pointing backward
and forward; or these turbaned
bathers, artful in Attic poses,
now look to us as innocent
as "Spring," arrayed here
as a disheveled shepherdess.

So intent is she on plucking
daisies from the field,
which seems to stretch out forever

beneath her flimsy satin shoes,
that she has forgotten
her blouse.

What can you do but unbutton
your coat and place it around
her shoulders? *Come along, Dear,*
you say, *put down your basket,*
and we'll have some tea. Come in
with me now, all of you,
for night is falling, and soon
you will be cold.

Stone Tool

For years it's been here on my desk,
the stone pestle the Salish woman
set down ten centuries ago
beside the cedar bowl and the waiting grain.
She must have heard her girl crying in the yard
or her man whistling up from the beach below
and set it down without thinking,
the way you set down a needle or a word,
as if it will actually wait for you—
not leap to the beak of some laughing bird
the minute your back is turned
or roll to your toddler's imperial hand
asking to be flung.

    And I can see this would have been
her best one, the shaft hewn by the rhythms
of laboring women, the head worn
smooth as beach rock by the tides
of the harvests.

    When they left camp it stayed behind,
a tuber of memory in the dark ground,
keeping its tale of feeding and plenty
until the morning my blue-eyed grandmother
turned over her spade,
and we laughed at the way a thing
disappears until it is ready to find you,
until it is hungry for use.

Post Hoc

It happened because he looked a gift horse in the mouth.
It happened because he couldn't get that monkey off his back.
It happened because she didn't chew 22 times before swallowing.
What was she *thinking*, letting him walk home alone from the bus stop?
What was he *thinking*, standing up in the boat like that?
Once she signed those papers the die was cast.
She should have waited an hour before going in; everyone knows
salami and seawater don't mix.
He should have checked his parachute a seventh time;
you can never be too careful.
Why didn't she declare her true feelings?
Why didn't she play hard to get? She could be out at some
nice restaurant right now instead of in church, praying
for the strength to let him go.
It all started with that tattoo.
It all started with her decision to order the chicken salad.
Why was he so picky?
Why wasn't she more discriminating?
He should have read the writing on the wall; listened
to the still small voice, had a lick of sense. But how could he when he
was blinded by passion? Deaf to warnings? Really dumb?
Why, *why*, in God's name, did he run with scissors?
If only they'd asked Jesus for help.
If only they'd asked their friends for help.
If only they'd ignored the advice of others and held fast
to their own convictions, they might all be here, now,
with us, instead of six feet under, instead of trying to adopt
that *foreign* baby, instead of warming that barstool
at the Road Not Taken Eatery and Lounge, wondering how it might all
have been different, if only they had done
the right thing.

three

Blue Yodel

They were the first physicians of woe,
those Delta Bluesmen, how skillfully they marked
the course of hard luck's chronic variations:
The Worried Blues, the Mean Mamma Blues,
the Bo'weavil or Backwater Blues, knowing
that even the Careless Love Blues is no happy fever,
that once exposed you could relapse forever,
the familiar strain of another's symptoms
enough to cause swelling, a phantom throb
at the site of an old infection;

                          the way that now,
just hearing Jimmie Rodgers on the radio singing
Miss the Mississippi and You is already taking you back—
the *plink plink plink* of his guitar filling the tin pail
of memory with the sound of rain on the roof
of your lost pine shack on the Mississippi,
where you sat on the porch with a line in the water,
or on the plank seat of your little boat, pulling your net
under the surface, then raising it to drip
in the sun;

                          so that this morning,
even its Northern rays, warm on your arm
as you drive to the cleaners, seem a kind of current
which has carried you slowly downstream
to where Rodgers sits strumming on the bank
in the same golden day, his straw hat pushed back
on his forehead, his kerchief knotted low
around his throat, the roiling syllables of a long
blue yodel swirling in the air, like the churning coil
where the River meets the Gulf.

                              How easily it carries
over the watery lifespan between you,
piercing the ear of the heart, which stirs
in its craggy hollow, remembering a boot,
a bottle cap—all the beautiful bright things
it swallowed whole—
the false promise of each shining lure,
the cold kiss of the hook.

I Call a Librarian in Riverside

(after Frank O'Hara)

to ask a question about Ezra Pound
for a paper I'm writing so I can get tenure
and maybe even a house with a tree
I've planted myself in the front yard
and a porch where I can drink soulful cocktails
in the uncritical light of a

                summer afternoon

the two most beautiful words in the English language
according to Henry James I tell him
my theory and we talk about The Archive
that's what I love about reference librarians
they know what you need better than you do
and they
            ACTUALLY HELP YOU FIND IT
So
while I don't know his name or his secret grief or whose bed
he slips his slippers under at night for a few minutes
we're galvanized: two sub-atomic particles sparking
and glowing
               in our arcane valence

and when we have found the answer our work done
what do we do but slip coolly back into the inert
substance of our elemental selves
pedantium or academium the odds

6.02×10^{23} to 1 against
meeting again he being in Riverside (Oh!) unless
in some simultaneous reverie of Venice on a summer

afternoon, strolling with Ezra—still both particle and wave

HIS SHOCKING HAIR TAMED!
into solemn poplars along the Cannaregio
the mad alchemy of his brain transmutating softly into
gold Venetian light.

The Poetry Birds

When a friend asks why I am not a novelist,
I lean back in my chair and watch the sky,
wondering how to tell him that although
I have combed the Gulf Coast towns
of my childhood, seeking the snowy egrets
of great short fiction, it is only the poetry birds
who land on me.

    And although I have sat in the dust
of Midwest highways, setting out all the carrion
of my life, I cannot lure the great turkey vulture
that roosts in the hair of novelists and whispers
in his sleep a tale that is spellbinding, a *tour de force*,
and based on a true story.

    The poetry birds are another thing.
One morning I look out and see them,
a dark alphabet against the sky. Then
I anoint my arms with suet, tie cherries
in my hair, and stand, very still,
in the back yard.

    Confusion of wings and yellow feet!

    They flock down and I wear them,
a ravenous black veil,
and when they have picked me clean,
they fly off one by one,
until I am just a woman standing alone
in the backyard, and they, a line
in the gathering blue.

Afternoon with Frank O'Hara

O Frank O'Hara O Frank O'Hara
where are you on this last day
of July when I have made tuna fish sandwiches
which are so good with these salty potato chips and blue
sky and geraniums.
          Sit down and we'll survey
the public dock next door where I have seen Walt Whitman
in a lawn chair by the bathhouse, an asphodel
in one hand, a chrome whistle in the other,
regarding these slim young men
in tiny bathing suits whose buckles—yes buckles!—
catch the sun. See how they climb the ladder
to the high dive and fall
          down, in an endless
            swan-dive-somersault-freestyle
          feedback loop.
Their faith astounds us, and their turn-taking insouciance,
for by such deeds human goodness is made plain.
Will you have a gimlet?
Did you get the heaven you wanted?
O stay until the moon extends its silver rungs down
to the lake and tell me once and for all
if it is better to be famous and dead or alive
and unknown.
          Too soon we shall step tipsi-
ly into my small canoe and row toward that shimmering trellis,
where swimmers of every description—strong and sure,
or ringed by inflatable sea monsters—are going up
and coming down.
          Then you'll step out,
the one dry suit on the teeming dais, and I'll watch you,

rising together, waving, and calling down like a blessing:
It's good to be alive and lonely—

and I'll feel it, flooding the North
and South of me, filling my fertile plains,
stretching Eastward and Westward
like my very own land.

Meditation from 14A

And what if the passage out of this life
is like a flight from Seattle to St. Louis—

the long taxi out of the body, the brief
and terrible acceleration, the improbable

buoyancy, and then the moment when,
godlike, you see the way things fit

together: the grave and earnest roads
with their little cars, stitching their desires

with invisible thread; the tiny pushpin houses
and backyard swimming pools, dreaming

the same blue dream. And who but the dead
may look down with impunity on these white

birds, strewn like dice above a river whose name
you have forgotten, though you know,

having crossed the Divide, that it flows
east now, toward the vast, still heartland,

its pinstriped remnants of wheat and corn
laid out like burial clothes. And how

you would like to close your eyes, if only
you could stop thinking about that small scratch

on the window, more of a pinprick, really,
and about yourself *sucked out!* anatomized!—

part of you now (the best part) a molecule
of pure oxygen, breathed in by the farmer

on his tractor; by the frightened rabbit
in the ditch; by a child riding a bike

in Topeka; by the sad wife of a Mexican
diplomat; by a dog, digging up a bone

a hundred years in the future, that foreign city
where you don't know a soul, but where you think

you could start over, could make a whole
new life for yourself, and will.

Postcard from the Moral High Ground

Doubtless in time you'll wish you were here,
wish you had persevered up the narrow

switchback trail to this high ridge,
where, I can report, the weather is clear,

without a trace of the mist that settles
in your little valley, in the cobbled lanes,

where villagers, their hair cut straight
across their foreheads, run around

in brown smocks, tipping cows
and looking for witches to dunk.

You may think you understand perspective,
but you don't—not until you've taken the long view,

fingered the wide thigh of the earth
up to the vanishing point.

It changes a person—it really does—
fills one with something like love, that extends,

as I write this, even to your lowland friends.
And who would not be moved to see them,

sticking their necks out over well-holes,
thanking the god who blinks back

for the invention of the fork,
for beer and onions at day's end,

for the shadow of night that leans lightly
against the walls of this cathedral town,

for the four-cornered world
on which it sleeps.

The Suicides

They turned up again this morning,
the suicides I've known—stepping
shyly out of the suburban woods
   to circle my campsite.

  Courteous they come, bearing
what they have before them:
the drowned cousin, large with child,
   a cup of water; the clowning uncle,

  the bullet he keeps hidden behind
his ear; the neighbors' son carries
his whole life ahead of him, piled high
   as laundry, tied with a noose.

  They come early, as always,
even the former student who loved
sleeping late, her backpack bursting
   with little pills, so many

  the dawn is pink with them.
Wary as wild dogs and clad in the fog
that clings to them, they gather on the lawn,
   neither glad nor sorry,

  to sit for a while by the small fire
I keep going with whatever burns.
They know it cannot warm them;
   they like its whispered cadences,

its flickering light; they delight
in the quick resurrection of sparks that die
into pure white ash, then rise, tiny angels
    drifting skyward.

In the City of Crows and Commuters

On hearing that Seattle has eclipsed Hartford as the crow capital of the world.

In the catalogue of quotidian wonders
this takes the cake: the five o'clock
convergence of freeway and flyway,
weekdays, in the city Arboretum.

Look up some October evening
and you'll see them, a million black
wings and urgent flapping shadows,
coming in so fast you'd think they'd set

the woods on fire. From the boughs
of their piney mothers, they look down
on the lawyers and moneymen winding
through the two-lane shortcut in the bellies

of their armored boxes, and laugh,
as two by two the yellow eyes blink on,
trying to scare back the night assembling
piece by piece overhead, cawing its

dusky victory, and the drivers,
if they notice at all, think *Where did all
these damned birds come from?* and roll on,
dreaming of supper in their own

drowsy houses. Rouse the neighbors;
they're not interested. History,
as usual, is looking the other way,
as two great nations under God

meet daily at the hour of returning,
with no anthem but the chord
of the long, blue day drawn back
behind them, no standard but the moon,
who stands at the screen door of evening
in her pale yellow apron, calling
and calling their names.

Modern Poetry

She comes to my office after class,
the pretty blond student, drawn
by the story I like to tell of one
who passed through years before,
the boy who so loved Sylvia Plath that,
despondent after three pints
at a Hebden pub, he lay down on her grave
and slept happily till dawn, when the tip
of an old woman's walking stick fell
and pierced his dreaming.

    Do you believe in soul mates? she asks,
her eyes two sharpened spades
turning the loam of her future.
I watch it bloom in the space between us:
I see two A-student English majors,
the little house, the sunny patio; I see
his long, muscled body stretched out
on top of her, and the children,
happy rootlings, trunk and limb,
safe in Spring's green intention. *I mean,*
since we both love her so much—

    Then, a rumbling, as underground
the red tap root awakens, ravenous,
bleeding her toxins. *I just thought . . .*
she smiles, and now I cannot stop
the slow, systemic blight—
the first affair, black spot and claw vine,
the thrum of locusts, rasping their litanies.

Loosed they will devour everything.

. . . well, who knows what could happen?
I see the smoking pit where the house
had stood, the blistered stalks,
the posted warnings. Yes, yes, I say,
of course, and write down his name.
There, I say, now *run.*

My Father's Platitudes

I'm in the kitchen slicing bread for a sandwich
when he starts in again, my dead father, with his advice;
only it's not his treatise on how we should all listen
to Thor Heyerdahl, who was a true genius and not the crackpot
everybody said he was, or why I should swap the IBM
for pure gold bullion on account of the Jews.

One day death will catch up to other technology
and the words of the dead sail effortless through dry space,
but now they arrive random as coconuts,
sodden as crated wreckage.

I watch him waving from the shore, making big
hand signals, like castaways in the movies.
It's me, he calls, *your everlovin' father,*
and he looks okay, though not as I remember him,
young in dress whites and epaulettes,
or later, skeletal on a raft of empty bottles,
his soul tied to the mast like a soiled undershirt.

I'm slicing a tomato at the equator, like he taught me.
A dull knife's more dangerous than a sharp one, he shouts,
sawing his hand back and forth in the air. I test the blade
with my thumb, thinking about knives and danger,
about what I would defend with my life.

ARE YOU A MAN OR A MOUSE, GODDAMMIT! he yells,
mixing me up with my brother, but I have theories
of my own, and I tell him that even mice have their share
of timid glory, outwitting the amber eye that's stalking them,
carrying crumbs home to the little ones, not crawling
into some rat hole to die.

Well, life is a shit sandwich, he says, holding it out
to me like spoils from a doomed vessel.
That's a good one, I say, and take it as my portion,
his gift from the fathomless reaches between us.

I'll Be Seeing You

Any day now it will happen:
three solemn knocks at the front door
and there you'll be, your shroud,
jaunty over one shoulder, your hair,
matted with sticks and leaves.

I didn't know you were dead, I'll say,
and you'll laugh, shaking the birdcage
of your bones till your heart rolls
like a stiffened locust.

And maybe I'll think how
you don't look so bad, even now,
with that beard the color of parched sod,
two hollow eyes like measuring spoons.

You knew I'd come, you'll whisper,
your toe creeping toward the threshold,
and I'll think how now, even dead women
aren't safe around you.

Touch me, you'll say, and I'll know,
even as my fingers open toward you,
that you'll never be content to moan down
my corridors and play havoc with my toaster;

you're there to coax me out. And though
your touch is a cool transfusion of darkness,
and my skin looks lovely poppied with bruises,
and the light now slices like glass—

I'll shut the door and turn back to life,
who has fallen asleep in the next room
watching television, his plaid bathrobe open,
tomorrow's newspaper slipping
from his hand.

Poem by Numbers

We murder to dissect.
—WORDSWORTH

In the foreground we see the barn in sunlight,
rendered here in the Deep Cadmium
of country dahlias, except for this shaded trapezoid
in Red Oxide, the precise color of dried blood.

And to the left, the dark mosaic of the old sycamore,
its bark flecked here and there with Copper,
like a rusted sling blade, its leaves burnished
in Umber and Sepia, hinting, always, at the

dead weight of summer, eased only,
in this composition, by the cool invitation
of the Viridian lake. The sky, in contrast,
is a pure and haughty Cerulean, a shade
that gives up nothing, like the beautiful witness
who doesn't want to get involved.

Note that the canvas contains no trace of yellow,
a color which, as everyone knows,
increases nervous agitation, and which, at any rate,
would surely detract from the happy children—

the Titanium dabs of their frocks suggesting
innocence and motion—running, as they are,
through the Ochre grasses of late afternoon,
into the barn through the open door,

indicated here by a definitive slice
of True Black, a shade that devours light
as the watching eye devours the good
and bleeds it into words.

The School of Weeping

At Mater Dolorosa Elementary, the nuns,
gray and obedient as banded doves,
waited on the Lord, as we waited on recess.

Pope Paul VI and General Washington squared off
over the dented globe, but the true center
was the marble Virgin, mindless, always,

of the twisted serpent under her bare, left foot,
its forked tongue limp as a hair ribbon.
All day she stared down from her niche

in the hall, grieving for our sins, we knew,
and missing her Son, crucified, and married
to our teachers. We wondered

if he came to them in the night, their tardy
Bridegroom, touching the stiff white gowns
we'd spied swaying

on the line behind the convent, leaving tender,
bloody fingerprints to be scrubbed out
in the morning before Social Studies.

Each May we made altars for our sad Mother,
carrying lilacs from home to cheer her up
a bit, yet knowing, finally,

there was nothing we could do,
any more than for our own moms, who worked
swing shift in the hospital laundry,

or sat sobbing in the basement with a stack
of 45s and a sixpack. So we knelt on the cool,
waxed floor beside our desks at the end

of the day, inching around the rosary, reciting
the angel's greeting—*Hail Mary, Full of Grace*—
over and over, the way grownups

told their good stories again and again for laughs,
our eyes closed, trying as best we could to shut out
the melody of the purple ice cream truck

that careened up and down Felicity Street on warm
spring days, blaring "Pop Goes the Weasel," daring
us out into the green, hysterical world.

Jeffrey Dahmer's Father

I heard him on the radio this afternoon,
trying to understand how his son could have
turned out that way, reaching for an explanation,
like a man trying to climb out of the sea.
A chemist, he kept slipping back
to the methods of his craft, seeking the dark
variable that could neutralize a father's love,
contaminate the clear distillation of summers
at the lake, the spring they raised lambs in Ohio.
"There were a lot of activities," he says, finally,
"but nothing ever took, so he never bonded
with people." Someone has told him this,
and he says it like a man poring over and over
familiar calculations, trying to fit them
to the severed head the son kept
in the strongbox, the limbs, preserved
in oil drums in his room—
seeking the wild, immeasurable trace
that could explain how, while the father
ordered worlds in glass containers,
the son supped on the genitals of lost boys
and left him reaching for the knotted rope
of his life.

Falling Asleep at the Wheel

All you know is you must get home—
   and 30 miles isn't so far, even on a country road,
even at midnight in the rain.

Next it is warm and easy, with Etta James
   on the radio singing, *At last my love has come along . . .*
the long notes taking you up and down, up

and down, over the glistening fields, and like Etta
   you have never been so happy, the miles
falling away behind you like a dream.

And when the doe appears at the bend
   in the road, her eyes a red signal flare,
willingly you turn and follow,

into the silent woods, over the creek
   to her mossy bed,
where a lean man waits in the dark,

and you feel his desire, thick in the night air
   and yourself already yielding—
though there is something holding you

back, something half-remembered,
   a line you must not cross.
At laaaast, he says, the word blossoming out and out

filling the distance between you like forever
   and you know how good it would be—
the hard push, the catch

of breath—you know he would never hurt you
    and you want him—his arms opening
wide now O God, *you want him*

you want him his white eyes two
    stars *falling fast—so fast—*
        to meet you

The Mergansers

Even their name recalls some comic
misalliance in an old T.V. show, and when
I see them on the lake this morning,
I want to go up to her privately,
to the female, wearing her beige breast
like a spotted housecoat, and whisper
at the side of her red, Phyllis Diller head crest,
into the ear hole that must be there somewhere,
the advice my mother gave me at fifteen:
Never trust a man who's prettier than you are.

Of course she meant Danny Scarlati,
who worked that summer on the neighbors'
garage, a copy of Ovid in his jeans pocket.
Even then I understood his beauty
was a wound he'd spend his life avenging,
and when he turned to me, on a flat rock
after swimming, the water sparkling on him
like drops of precious metal, the heat rising
in me like smoke from a burning sacrifice,
I knew at once that it could really happen—
that God could drop down in feathered glory
and force some maiden like that
in his terrible beak, and out of the egg
could come this boy—half man, half god—
with this broad back, this eye trained
on the lake and sky.

The male is preening some distance off;
the sun touches his sleek head, his glossy wings,
making his colors come. As soon as the eggs

are laid, he'll take off for the coast. Maybe
he'll tell her the one about the pack of cigarettes,
or about his cousin who has a job for him
in L.A., and disappear into a sky as clear
and hard as the back window of a '69 Impala.
Then she'll look down astonished
to see herself, a new creature in sandals
and a halter top, standing at the edge
of the driveway, the moon rising pale
as an eggshell against all the sky
behind her.

Other Books in the Crab Orchard Series in Poetry

Muse
Susan Aizenberg

Lizzie Borden in Love:
Poems in Women's Voices
Julianna Baggott

This Country of Mothers
Julianna Baggott

White Summer
Joelle Biele

In Search of the Great Dead
Richard Cecil

Twenty First Century Blues
Richard Cecil

Circle
Victoria Chang

Consolation Miracle
Chad Davidson

Names above Houses
Oliver de la Paz

The Star-Spangled Banner
Denise Duhamel

Beautiful Trouble
Amy Fleury

Pelican Tracks
Elton Glaser

Winter Amnesties
Elton Glaser

Always Danger
David Hernandez

Fabulae
Joy Katz

Train to Agra
Vandana Khanna

For Dust Thou Art
Timothy Liu

Strange Valentine
A. Loudermilk

American Flamingo
Greg Pape

Crossroads and Unholy Water
Marilene Phipps

Birthmark
Jon Pineda

Year of the Snake
Lee Ann Roripaugh

Misery Prefigured
J. Allyn Rosser

Roam
Susan B. A. Somers-Willett

Becoming Ebony
Patricia Jabbeh Wesley